ENDC

MW00415682

For the nearly three decades I have known Scott and Nancy Hinkle, they have never wavered from their passion and call to spread the gospel. I have known them, spoken at their conferences for radical outreach and evangelism, and have been their pastor.

As you read *Surprised*, you will be encouraged by how God takes broken lives and people such as Scott, restores them, and raises them up to reach so many others.

The dream and call God has placed upon Scott's life may very well affect you to the point of believing God to move you into the realm of the divine unexpected, making a greater difference than you ever imagined in the world you live in.

*Tommy Barnett*
*Global Pastor, Dream City Church Phoenix*
*Co-Pastor, Los Angeles Dream Center*


*Surprised* is the dramatic autobiography of a dedicated, passionate, and bold leader. Scott Hinkle is a remarkable man. Here in *Surprised*, he shares the life-changing story of how God brought him from devastation to peace and true purpose.

*Steve Robinson*
*Senior Pastor, Church of the King*
*Mandeville, LA*

This book by Scott Hinkle, *Surprised,* will open your heart and vision to see new possibilities and experience new and exciting adventures in your life. We were not meant to live a boring and purposeless life. From his own personal experience with God, Scott shares how the Lord opened up amazing opportunities as he surrendered his life to Him. And then he communicates clearly how God will do the same for you!

I have known Scott Hinkle for over twenty years and have watched him in action equip the church to live for and fulfill the Great Commission. He is a lover of Jesus, faithful and committed to his family, a man of character, and a very good friend of mine. I highly recommend his new book and his ministry to you.

*Greg Mohr*
*Executive Director of Education*
*Charis Bible College*
*Woodland Park, CO*


I have witnessed Pastor Scott Hinkle diligently serve God for decades. *Surprised* offers so much real-life experience to anyone on a lifelong journey serving God in a real way. Reading parts of Pastor Scott's journey that he has never shared before was so encouraging. This book will greatly help anyone at any stage of your Christian walk.

*Pastor Matthew Barnett*
New York Times *Best-Selling Author*
*Co-Founder of the Dream Center*

There are those life-altering relationships that God brings into your life that are a constant reminder of His heart for us; Scott Hinkle has been one of those in my life. He walks in the office of a true evangelist and his life testimony has not only encouraged me through the years but challenged me to live out the heartbeat of God for souls. I have watched him remain faithful to his calling and his responsibility to "equip the Church for the work of ministry" (Ephesians 4:12).

This book, *Surprised*, will reach into the depths of your heart and speak "life-giving principles" that have been the bedrock of the life of this man of God. It will take you back to your first encounter with Jesus ... or prayerfully lead you on a path to find Him for the first time. I pray that as you read this "testimony of the Lord," you will find yourself surprised at all God has in store for you!

*Rusty Nelson*
*Lead Pastor*
*The Rock Family Worship Center*
*Huntsville, AL*

# Scott Hinkle

Foreword by Nicky Cruz

# Surprised

## Living Life in the Unexpected

Published by:
R.H. Publishing
3411 Preston Rd. Ste C-13-146
Frisco, TX. 75034

ISBN#978-1-945693-52-6     paperback
ISBN#978-1-945693-53-3     eBook

Cover Design by Don Day

Edited by Carol Brown Patterson


Printed in the United States of America

# ACKNOWLEDGMENTS

Words fail to express the gratitude in my heart for the greatest gifts God could ever give me, not only in the writing of this project but in life. These gifts are at the center of the best parts of the journey. My wife, Nancy, the love of my life, and I have navigated victories and challenges along the pathways and highways of this great life mission. Our son Donovan, our daughter Stephanie Delgado with her husband Danny, and their boys, Jakson and Nikolas, have all added fullness of life and joy along the way.

I've learned that God's greatest gifts to us this side of heaven are people. Without others — such as friends, family, pastors, or co-laborers — we would walk alone. Without those whom Jesus allows us to touch and reach, our lives would be without purpose.

A special thanks to a great team who helped pull this all together — Carol Brown Patterson, Don Day and Polly Harder.

I'm grateful for every life whose path we've crossed. You have made this book possible. Thank you!

# FOREWORD

Scott Hinkle is driven by an unquenchable passion for souls. I have known him and his wife, Nancy, as friends and co-laborers for many, many years, so I am not surprised that Scott is writing this new book!

The word "surprise" comes to us through Latin and eventually French and has a meaning of an unexpected attack or capture, or to be seized by something or someone. Knowing Scott's and Nancy's background and testimony, I know for a fact that they weren't expecting to be set free by the love and power of Jesus, yet here they are! I know that I wasn't expecting anything except to be hated, rejected and to die a violent death — but, surprise, surprise, Jesus found me by sending a laborer, David Wilkerson, to reach me with the message that Jesus loved me.

I know and expect that you might feel that your life is too broken, too irredeemable to be used by the Lord to reach the lost. But God's ways are not our ways. He uses the broken and the most unlikely and offers us the opportunity to become involved in the most important mission in all of creation — to love and follow Him, and to be a voice crying in the wilderness to reach the broken and abandoned. The need is enormous.

I am convinced that as you read *Surprised* and allow His Holy Spirit to impregnate you with a burden for the lost, you will be seized and captured by the love of God and by His calling — the highest calling — to dedicate yourself to something eternal. Nothing really matters in this life other than knowing Jesus and saying yes to His call.

*Nicky Cruz*
*Evangelist, Author*
*Colorado Springs, CO*

# TABLE OF CONTENTS

# PREFACE

In every generation there exists an enormous need — matched by an immeasurable opportunity — for God to raise up men and women to represent Him in every area of life.

Great institutions of learning prepare those who respond to His invitation to join Him in spreading the life only Jesus can bring.

The road to following Jesus is filled with turns, mountains, valleys and more — most of which are unexpected.

Whom God chooses and the path He designs to raise them up is always interesting. Many people have a Christian background, come up through the church community ranks, and find a place of serving the King. Others, today, come from a background of brokenness without a trace of Christian influence. They are being transformed by the Holy Spirit and used by God. Jesus develops men and women for His use on personally designed paths so they may fulfill His great purpose for their lives.

This book has three major parts. The first unfolds portions of my personal story. The second relays a way God may call us. The third includes some life-lived and proven principles to help better define God's working in a person's life.

Rest assured that God's way is filled with surprises! And this makes Christianity anything but boring.

My prayer for you as you read this journey through the highways of my life and, more importantly, the truth of His Word is that you will embrace God's surprises and call so you might know that your life counts more than you ever dreamed.

# Section One

# Chapter 1

# "I WAS SURPRISED!"

Have you ever been to a high school reunion? Such gatherings are often great places to experience the unexpected.

You might remember those years in high school. There were those students nobody really noticed. Maybe they were the not too social type, the super studious kind who passed through the halls without making so much as a ripple. As time went by, their teen-age years faded away and they developed into personal or business successes without a trace of their high school appearance. Surprise!

Of course, there were those classmates who looked like they

were popular and had it "all together." You were just sure something great was going to take place in their future. Yet what takes place falls far short of the early great expectations. Surprise again!

I once attended a high school reunion. It was great to reconnect with so many I had known during those formative and often fun years. Graduates from this class came from literally all over America to participate. Some had become very accomplished in their field.

As we all were standing in the banquet hall, close to the wall, a former classmate looked at me and said, *"I heard you were a minister."*

My reply was simply, "Yes!"

He quickly exclaimed, *"I was surprised."*

I responded even more quickly, *"So am I."*

I'll share more backstory on this particular surprise later on.

You see, when you choose to follow Christ, you can rest assured your life will be filled with the unexpected and great surprises that He has a habit of bringing about.

He literally does *"exceedingly abundantly above all that we ask or think"* (Ephesians 3:20).

Following is a poem I wrote shortly after my conversion:

*From the street to the penthouse suite*
*From the bar to the limousine car*
*People are dyin' and going to hell.*

*From Moscow to L.A.*
*Many will loudly say,*
*I wish my life would come quickly to an end.*

*So there's one thing I've gotta ask*
*And it might put a crack in your mask.*

*Do you care, Christian?*
*Do you even care?*

*People go to hell by a countless score.*
*We don't blink an eye when there's more and more.*
*All we pray is, God, bless me and mine.*
*Do you care, Christian? Do you even give a hoot?*

*Could you share Christ with one in need*
*Without being driven by a boot — Scoot!*

*Jesus loves you and so do I*
*His coming is very nigh.*

# Chapter 2

# "IT ALL STARTS HERE"

On March 17, crowds were celebrating Saint Patrick's Day on the famed Jersey Shore. Twenty-seven-year-old Bernice Lesser Hinkle was about to give birth to her first-born son by caesarean delivery. There were potential complications. Her womb was filled with tumors and the doctor was contemplating the possibility of making a choice between saving the mother or the child. Yet at 12:15 p.m. a 5-pound, 13-ounce boy, Scott Alan Hinkle, was born at Fitkin Hospital (today Jersey Shore Medical Center) in Neptune, New Jersey.

Hopes were high for this first-born Jewish son. My mother, Bernice, had been a stenographer at Ft. Monmouth, New Jersey, and my father, Lee, a decorated, Bronze Star WWII soldier, was a civilian instructor in Radar and later Satellite Communications at the Army base as well.

With my childhood dreams of going to either Julliard School of Music (I played trumpet and drums) or Princeton University to become a lawyer on the path of following my boyhood idol, Abraham Lincoln, in becoming President of the United States, my future surely did look bright.

While in middle school I began to get attention by cutting up in class, which led to spending time in the principal's office. Upon graduation from the eighth grade, my family moved about four miles away from Eatontown (near the Army base) to Oakhurst, New Jersey. While that may not seem far away (New Jersey being the most densely populated state in the country), it was a whole new world for me.

Feeling the social pressure of being a new student in a new town, I soon realized I did not fit in with the crowd in the college prep courses. I was more attracted to those who wore black leather jackets and were called "hoods." They looked "cool" and seemed to have more fun. Following along this path, doing what they did, I began to drink cheap wine, hang out on the streets in the oceanfront communities of Asbury Park and Bradley Beach, and became part of that crowd. Before long, I went from just drinking to smoking pot and taking pills, usually barbiturates (called downers).

One summer evening I had gone to a doctor and obtained a

prescription for Nembutal (a barbiturate) under false pretenses. By the time I got back to my friends, I had taken several tablets. They were supposed to be taken over a period of time and the number I took caused me to overdose. My friends laid me in an alley off Main St. in Bradley Beach and left me there, with little regard for my welfare. Later I awoke and made my way home. The crowd I ran with was also using heroin and when I was sixteen, I began to shoot heroin. Lying, scheming, stealing, and buying drugs immediately became the focal point of my life. All I wanted to do was get more dope, take another fix, and get high — nothing else mattered. This led to brushes with the law and persistent trouble in school.

On a December day, a friend named Anthony (name has been changed) asked me to score (buy) heroin for him and his friend. Knowing there could be some profit from this, I took Anthony and his friend to a drug dealer where they could buy whatever they wanted. Two months later, in the middle of a cold night in February, the police came to my parents' home, where I was living. The officers got me out of bed and searched my room. They then arrested me on the charges of aiding and abetting the sale of heroin and possession of a controlled substance and took me to the county jail.

My "friend" Anthony had set me up to buy drugs for an undercover narcotics agent and I was arrested as part of an area-wide drug bust with over one hundred arrests. I was not allowed to return to high school and became one of the first students ever put out for drugs. I was admitted to a psychiatric ward for forty days and later went to court.

Beginning with this arrest, God put into motion a series of events to salvage my life from sure destruction The extreme downward spiral of my life had already surprised my family, who watched my childhood dreams of attending Julliard in New York City and Princeton University disappear. My aspirations of becoming a musical performer and lawyer evaporated, replaced by the reality that jail time was possibly facing me. After agreeing to a plea bargain, I was required to leave the state of New Jersey and live with relatives in Kansas. I also had to continue psychological treatment and return to high school.

Soon after arriving in western Kansas, I resumed my life of partying, drinking, and using drugs. On one occasion, when my aunt and uncle were out of town, I made a quick trip in and out of New Jersey to buy drugs. When my uncle discovered this escapade, he immediately put me on a plane back to New Jersey.

Another of my father's brothers offered to help me and he took me into his family's home in central Kansas. As soon as I arrived, I began to go through withdrawals from heroin.

I enrolled in the local high school and became disruptive on my first day of class, arguing with the teacher and getting into trouble. The pattern of drug use continued.

# Chapter 3

## "A HAIRPIN TURN"

On Tuesday morning, March 24, one week after I turned nineteen, the high school had an anti-drug assembly in the first hour. My distant cousin, Pat, and I were sitting in the balcony of the gymnasium listening to the speaker, Charles McPheeters. McPheeters was a former drug user and rock musician from Hollywood. His presentation consisted of his firsthand story, which was both personal and humorous. He recounted dramatic events of his life, including his near-fatal drug overdose and the radical change that came into his life when he was set free from drugs.

I had no real interest in listening to the speaker because I thought I already knew everything about using drugs. I actually began to make up reasons why I didn't want to listen to what he was saying. But then something happened! I heard a voice speak to me — not a loud, booming audible voice, but a voice on the inside, like a whisper — saying, *"Hinkle, listen to this guy. He has something to say ... you don't know everything."*

I began to listen more with my heart than with my excuse-manufacturing mind. And as I listened, a ring of truth went off in my heart and I began to think, "I have to talk to this guy." Because of my interest in music, I thought maybe that could be a connection. After asking one of the school officials about McPheeters' schedule, I borrowed a car from my cousin and began to follow him. This in itself was a small miracle, because under normal circumstances, my cousin never would have let me borrow anything, let alone his car.

The assembly session was already over by the time I reached the first school, but I found out where the next school was (about nine miles further west in another town) and I continued on, determined to talk to McPheeters. Walking into the high school gym in the middle of this next assembly, heads turned my way. This was a small town and I appeared in their midst with long hair, a pierced ear, scraggly beard, bell-bottom jeans and a striped shirt — very obviously an outsider.

I was asked to leave the premises, so I went out into the parking lot to wait for McPheeters. A 1969 red and white Super Sport Malibu Chevrolet with New York license plates caught my eye, and I quickly recognized its occupant as Judy McPheeters. Her husband had introduced her at the school assembly earlier that morning.

Hesitantly I walked over to the car and peered in. Through the window I could see little red stickers on the dashboard that read, "Jesus loves you." When Judy rolled down the window and spoke to me, I saw that she was reading her Bible. One of the first things I noticed was that her Bible had been underlined. My immediate thought was, "That's pretty sacrilegious." I recalled an article I had read about Jesus Freaks. It said they lived in communes in the hills, surrounded by trees and mud. I had absolutely no knowledge of Christianity, although I had been brought up in the most highly educated, densely populated, politically and economically powerful part of America (the Northeast). I was as unreached and unchurched as anyone in a dark, remote jungle on another continent.

Charles McPheeters came out of the school gym and joined his wife. I had brought along a friend, and we were both surprised when they invited us to join them for lunch at the local A&W Root Beer stand. The four of us went inside and he bought me a hamburger, french fries and soda. While we were eating, Charles asked me to go out to the car with him and Judy remained inside talking to my friend.

Charles and I sat in the front seat of the car, and he opened the Bible and began to read. As he shared about Christ's life-changing power, something began to happen inside me. I began to feel uncomfortable — I immediately knew that using profanity was wrong — and I realized my life was a mess. It wasn't so much the words I was hearing, but I had met someone who had Jesus in his life and wasn't afraid to show it. The evidence was shining through and having a direct effect on me.

As I sat there in the front seat of that Malibu, I bowed my head and silently cried out in my heart, *"God, if You can do everything this guy is talking about, then go on ahead and do it. It's either You or the gutter for me, and I've been in the gutter. I am out of options."* Immediately, I felt as if Someone had come in on the inside of me. All I could imagine was a man in painter's coveralls, with a scrub brush and a hose cleaning me out from the inside. It was as if all the crud was draining out of my life. I felt brand new!

Charles gave me a paperback Amplified New Testament and a handful of literature and told me about a white, wood-framed church on the edge of the town I lived in.

After that life-altering encounter with Jesus in the parking lot, I went back to Great Bend and ran into a friend standing with his girlfriend outside the high school. The first words out of my mouth were, *"I just asked Jesus into my life! I don't have to do drugs anymore. Don't knock Him until you try Him!"* From that very moment I was drafted by heaven into a lifetime journey and adventure of telling the world, *"Jesus Christ will change your life!"*

When I returned to school the next day, the principal questioned me about why I had skipped classes the day before. I shared with him what had happened and explained that I had asked Jesus to come into my life. The principal looked at me and solemnly replied, "This day will represent a hairpin turn in your life!"

Three days later, I was invited to go to a local church's youth retreat. This was an entirely new experience for me. It was being held in a retreat house for the Girl Scouts and a local evangelist was speaking. As I stood in the back listening to the message, the speaker gave the invitation to go forward. I went forward and followed the instructions being given.

He said, "Get down on your knees" and I did.

"Lift up your hands as if lifting up the entirety of your life to Jesus" and I did this, too.

Pray this prayer: "*Lord, here's my life, the good and the bad. Do with it what You will. I will go where You would have me to go; I will say what You would have me to say; I will do what You would have me to do, and I will be what You would have me to be. In Jesus' name. Amen.*"

God was listening as I entered into serving the King of kings! Immediately, I began to tell my friends about Christ, and I also began going out onto the streets of this small Kansas town, witnessing wherever I could. I became part of a ministry headed up by the local evangelist, and I even moved in with him and his family. I became part of the "little white, wood-framed church," which was just a few blocks away in walking distance from where I lived.

Called Faith Community Church, it was pastored by Fred and Sally Kirkpatrick, who had helped pioneer the Charismatic Movement in that area. A few weeks after meeting Christ in the parking lot, I was taken to a retreat in the Kansas City area, where I was brought to a David Wilkerson Crusade at Kemper Arena. When I responded to the altar call to make a public profession of my newfound faith, I reconnected with Charles McPheeters, who was serving as an altar worker.

Soon, Pastor Kirkpatrick allowed me to gather up all my old friends in the church's Fellowship Hall for an impromptu meeting. I wanted to tell them what had happened to me and explain how the same could happen to them. As I spoke, I finished everything I had to say in about three minutes and then repeated myself in about another minute and a half. I had fully expected to be able to preach a dynamic message, but I fell completely short of my expectations — which was extremely embarrassing!

Looking over to the side of the room, I saw the door that opened to the outside and quickly exited the building. Running down the street, I was thinking that I would never do that ever again. A precious lady from the church, Sister Joanne, ran down the street after me and brought me back inside. By this time, the pastor had finished speaking to the gathering.

The Charismatic Renewal and the Jesus Movement were in full swing at this time. Doors began to open for me to share my story and testimony in churches, retreats, Bible studies, Christian business groups, and other gatherings. In spite of my earlier disappointment at public speaking, I continued to tell how Jesus had changed my life. Again, I went out on the streets sharing my testimony with others. The call of God had become immediately real after that parking lot encounter with Jesus Christ.

## A SUPERNATURAL SURPRISE

With my growing involvement in the local area and meeting other Christians, I developed a new circle of friends. I had met some other Christian young people in the Wichita area, and I visited them on the campus of Wichita State University. As I walked onto the campus something dramatic happened. I saw the flames of hell before me, and I could hear the cries of those who were perishing.

The message was clear! There is only one way to avoid this eternal destruction and that is through Jesus Christ. I knew I had to spread the Good News of Jesus Christ!

## THE CALL CONTINUES TO GROW

Although I was still living in Kansas, Charles McPheeters, the young evangelist who had led me to Christ, kept in touch with me. After about a year, I reconnected with Charles and Judy. They were holding meetings in towns across America as they made their way to California where they planned to launch an outreach in Hollywood. There was a great need for evangelism there, so I packed up and joined them.

During the summer months they continued to minister, and I shared the testimony of my miraculous deliverance from drugs. It was a thrill to be part of a Jesus Festival, being held on the fairgrounds in Salt Lake City that summer.

One night I was asked to bring the evangelistic message and give the altar call. I spoke on Matthew 11:28:

> *"Come to Me, all you who labor and are heavy*
> *laden, and I will give you rest."*

This was my first actual evangelistic sermon — and several responded to the altar call for salvation.

During that summer, Charles told me of a new Bible college in Dallas, Texas — Christ For The Nations Institute. Knowing God's call was on my life, I wanted more training for ministry, so I headed to Texas. Going to the heart of the Bible Belt in Dallas was a whole new religious, cross-cultural experience, filled with challenges and surprises. I had never been around so many churches, religious organizations, and Christian-type people.

During my first semester at Christ For The Nations Institute, I spent some time in the prayer room at the Christian Center building on campus. During one such prayer time, a Scripture reference was brought clearly to mind. The reference was unfamiliar to me, so I looked it up and read,

> *"And Jesus went about all Galilee, teaching in their synagogues, preaching the gospel of the kingdom, and healing all kinds of sickness and all kinds if disease among the people" (Matthew 4:23).*

This word from God through the Scripture confirmed and underscored His call upon my life to travel and preach the gospel. After completing the first-year program at CFNI (I later completed a second year), I headed to Denver to help Charles launch The Holy Ghost Repair Service (HGRS) ministry to the streets of Denver. The eastern slope of the Rockies was flooded with hippies, drugs and radical movements, and Denver and Boulder were focal points.

The HGRS rapidly developed into a multi-faceted outreach that included The Paraclete Book & Music Store; Planet Jerusalem Coffee House; twice weekly JC University Bible studies; End Times Newspaper; Jesus Nite Patrol Street Witnessing; Love Lines Telephone Hotline; The Holy Ghost Repair Service Jesus 'Lectric Rock Band (I played drums); concert outreach rallies; and a daily radio show. At its peak, the ministry had volunteers and paid staff that numbered 35-40 people. I later became the assistant director.

As the season for the HGRS ministry began to change, I packed up my 1966 Bel Air Chevy (it had been given to me). It had army blankets for seat covers and a mismatched red front fender on a blue car due to an accident. I was headed back to New Jersey to launch an evangelistic ministry, and I preached some meetings in Michigan as I traveled across the country. I arrived back at the Jersey Shore and continued to preach wherever and whenever the opportunity arose.

As doors for ministry continued to open, I envisioned myself having cleaned up real well from the street-type look and life. I had been set free from that lifestyle and wanted to get as far away from the streets as I possibly could. I pictured myself becoming a great preacher, preaching nice sermons to nice people, and helping them get nicer. I soon felt as if the Lord spoke to me and said, *"That would be okay, but I'll have to call you by a different name — Jonah."*

I stopped in my tracks! Then I repented and wholeheartedly began to more fully embrace and follow God's call on my life. I knew I was called to reach the broken and hurting on the streets or wherever they were to be found. The desire of my heart was to bring the Gospel to as many people as possible who were just like I had been.

As time went by, the unfolding and walking out of my response to God brought many surprises.

# Section Two

# Chapter 4

# A SPECIAL GREAT SURPRISE

A pastor I had met in Kansas who now had a church in York, Pennsylvania, invited me to speak to his congregation. While I was there, he arranged for me to speak in a chapel service at a Christian drug rehabilitation ministry for women called New Life for Girls. It was founded by ex-drug addicts Demi and Cookie Rodriquez.

A short time later, I was invited to come on staff and serve as an assistant pastor at the church in York, and I also began to speak at New Life for Girls on a regular basis. After three months, I accepted an invitation to become the Academic Dean at the

New Life for Girls Training Center, where I coordinated three levels of Bible classes for a hundred women. Later, I became the meetings coordinator, which consisted of setting up meetings for Cookie Rodriquez. I was sent to David Wilkerson's ministry headquarters in Lindale, Texas, to be trained by his staff for this assignment.

One of the staff members at New Life for Girls and a former graduate of the program was a beautiful Italian girl named Nancy. She had come out of a background of drug addiction, gangs, and street life. I often represented New Life for Girls (NLFG) in churches, speaking, showing the movie, *The Cross and the Switchblade*, and presenting their ministry. Nancy was on the singing team from NLFG that accompanied me on these speaking engagements and we actually had our very first "date" on one of those ministry times.

Nancy's love for Jesus was what really caught my attention. And she was bold in her faith — she could pray, fight the devil, witness on the streets and preach the Gospel.

One day, while we were driving across the bridge over the Susquehanna River near Lancaster, Pennsylvania, I turned to Nancy and asked her to marry me — she said yes!

# Chapter 5

# AN UNLIKELY ARMY

Without a doubt, David was a renowned soldier who was known for his military victories. He even had a song that was sung about how he defeated the enemies of Israel:

> *"So the women sang as they danced, and said:*
> *'Saul has slain his thousands, and David his ten*
> *thousands'"* (1 Samuel 18:7).

Of course, this angered King Saul, who, overtaken by jealousy, persecuted and sought to kill David. David fled for his life and eventually came to a cave called Adullam.

> *"David therefore departed from there and*
> *escaped to the cave of Adullam. So when his*

39

*brothers and all his father's house heard it, they*
*went down there to him"* (1 Samuel 22:1).

When you are having a difficult time, it might be good to be around family, right? There is much more to this story.

*"And everyone who was in distress, everyone who*
*was in debt, and everyone who was discontented*
*gathered to him. So he became captain over*
*them. And there were about four hundred men*
*with him"* (1 Samuel 22:2).

What a crowd that must have been!

Imagine this! The king wants to find you and kill you. So you hide out in a cave and all your weird relatives — the debtor, the distressed, and the discontented — show up. If it happened today, the crowd might also include the depressed, diseased or drug addicted. For some reason they were drawn to David. In spite of it all, we read, *"David became their captain."*

The reason he became their captain was because he needed a fighting force and army. It doesn't sound as if many of these were what you might want to recruit for the military. Obviously, they were available but there has to be more to this. As we continue to track these men, we see that something unexpected took place. The debtors, the distressed and discontented became part of something else — David's mighty men! They became an elite fighting force, possibly much like our Marine Reconnaissance, Army Delta, Navy SEALS or Air Force PJs.

Obviously, something happened that transformed these men from the ragtag bunch at the cave of Adullam into a famous, superior group of soldiers, fighting alongside David winning tremendous victories. God gives us this great example of raising up an unlikely army to serve His purposes. He did it in David's time, and He has continued to do so even to this very day.

So, how does God change and raise up men and women today who might fit into "the cave of Adullam" profile?

1) BY FAITH. Some of us do not trust anyone. Trust issues have overtaken us. That must change — now. Our relationship with God is based on faith or belief, and I like to use the word trust as well.

   *"The just shall live by faith."* This statement is repeated four times in Scripture (see Romans 1:17; Galatians 3:11; Hebrews 10:38; Habakkuk 2:4). Obviously God has an important truth for us.

41

*"Without faith it is impossible to please Him, for he who comes to God must believe that He is, and that He is a rewarder of those who diligently seek Him"* (Hebrews 11:6).

You must trust Him with all your life — past, present and future. You trust that He can use your strengths and weaknesses as well as your victories and failures.

2) THE BLOOD. We want a new start — we wish the slate would be wiped clean. Through the work of Jesus Christ on the cross, the blood of Christ will cleanse our consciences, wipe away our sins, and break the ties of sin that have held our life captive.

*"But if we walk in the light as He is in the light, we have fellowship with one another, and the blood of Jesus Christ His Son cleanses us from all sin. If we say that we have no sin, we deceive ourselves, and the truth is not in us. If we confess our sins, He is faithful and just to forgive us our sins and to cleanse us from all unrighteousness"* (1 John 1:7-9).

Because of His shed blood on our behalf, we no longer are victims but victors.

3) THE WORD. God's Word — the Bible — is God's manual for life and the basis for truth. Read it every day. It is more valuable than music or cute quotes. Let it sink in and soak into your mind and heart.

*"How can a young man cleanse his way? By taking heed according to Your word"* (Psalm 119:9).

This applies to old men as well as young — and old women as well.

4) ACTION. The first action is to change — repent. Jesus said,
   *"Unless you repent you will all likewise perish"* (Luke 13:3).

True repentance is an attitude that leads to action.

Beyond this, as people of faith, we are also people of action. True biblical faith empowers us for action. We choose to intentionally pursue fulfilling God's purposes in our world.

*"But someone will say, 'You have faith, and I have works.' Show me your faith without your works, and I will show you my faith by my works"* (James 2:18).

We surrender to the call of God to be used as a vessel of life in a broken world.

# Chapter 6

# DIVINE SURPRISES

*"Our God is in heaven; He does whatever He pleases"* (Psalm 115:3).

Here is the bottom line. God is God … period. He can and does whatever He wants, through whomever He wants, and however He wants. He is God, and we are not. He created mankind, the earth, and the universe. God has an immeasurable track record of surprising His people and humanity.

Let's take a review.

The Bible is filled with surprising people.

As an infant, Moses was put into a basket and floated down the Nile River. He was rescued from the waters and raised in the home of Pharaoh. He lived as an Egyptian prince although he was a Hebrew. Then he murdered an Egyptian and was banished to the wilderness to live. He eventually became the deliverer of his people.

Surprise!

Joseph, the favorite son of his father, dreamed about everyone in his family bowing down to serve him. This insulted and angered his brothers, who then sold him off as a slave to Egypt. God's favor brought him to serve in the home of an Egyptian official, where he was falsely accused and ended up in prison. Yet, God again raised him up to become the second in command in Egypt and a type of messiah to his own family and people.

Another surprise.

Of course, there is also David. His father, Jesse, did not initially acknowledge him when Samuel came to his house to anoint the next king. King Saul didn't think this young fellow could fight Goliath. David, being just a shepherd and musician (not a certified ninja, giant-killing warrior) as well as short of physical stature, slayed the giant and became king of Israel. From him came the lineage for the Messiah.

Super surprise!

Let's look at more modern surprises in our own nation.

At the turn of the twentieth century, the outpouring of the Holy Spirit paved the way for Spirit-filled Christianity as we know it today. The results of this revival are still felt. I'm referring to the Azusa Street revival in Los Angeles. It did not begin in a stadium or fine auditorium with great music, dramatic lighting, big screens, popular preachers or religious power brokers.

It began in a house on Bonnie Brae Street, and continued in a building described by a Los Angeles newspaper as a "tumble down shack." The "leader" was a man with one eye named William Seymour. As an African-American, he'd been the victim of racial discrimination, and according to Frank Bartleman, *"Brother Seymour generally sat behind two empty shoe boxes, one on top of the other. He usually kept his head inside of the top one during the meeting, in prayer."*

During the World War I era, a baseball player from the Chicago White Sox named Billy Sunday, who had come from poverty, got saved and began to hold crusades across America with astounding results. He preached the Gospel as well as confronted the evils of the day. In New York City alone, there were 98,000 reported conversions to Christ.

The Roaring Twenties was a time of economic prosperity with a distinctive cultural edge in the United States, according to Wikipedia. In 1923, Aimee Semple McPherson, a barnstorming evangelist, broke ground for a building, stating the Lord told her, "If you dig a hole, I will fill it."

Angelus Temple was the church building and from this was launched an amazing church and ministry that gave birth to the worldwide Foursquare denomination. Salvations and healings took place and over one million people were fed in Los Angeles during the Great Depression through Angelus Temple. The ministry continues today and has a far-reaching impact under the leadership of Matthew Barnett and in partnership with the Dream Center.

Another divine surprise!

Following World War II there was a two-edged unleashing of power from heaven. The miracle and healing revivals were making a huge Pentecostal impact with men such as Oral Roberts, Jack Coe, and William Branham, along with Gordon Lindsay and The Voice of Healing. Many of these men came from poor and even uneducated backgrounds but they yielded to God. There were also three evangelists breaking onto the scene holding great meetings. Two of them flamed out quickly, and the third, thought by some to be the least talented, continued on.

His name — Billy Graham.

Again — surprise!

The gang leader of a vicious street gang called the Mau Maus in New York City, who was filled with hatred, born into poverty, spiritism and abuse in Puerto Rico, had his life radically transformed by Jesus Christ. His name is Nicky Cruz, and he has shared his story and preached the Gospel to over 50 million people worldwide. Another of God's wonderful surprises!

During the Vietnam era, America was torn apart politically, socially, and morally. The post-war, baby boom generation was coming of age and pushing the social and moral boundaries as far as possible with rebellion, drugs, free love and more. The self-destruct button had been pushed on this generation. Yet, heaven responded with a double-barreled surprise outpouring.

There was the Charismatic Renewal — affecting dead, dry and historical churches with the baptism of the Holy Spirit and an emphasis on teaching believers from the Bible. This outpouring even affected many Roman Catholics — to the chagrin of some Pentecostals. This could be called a revival.

Running a parallel time track was the more forceful and jagged-edged Jesus Movement. An entire segment of disenfranchised, drug using, immoral and rebellious lost youth were swept into the Kingdom of God, bringing about much needed and great church culture change. So many were surprised!

A move of God may thoroughly interrupt or upset the systems or practice of dead, dry, or entertainment-driven, nonlife-transforming, shallow imitations of Christianity. Awakening and revival can be looked at as God interrupting normal religion with an invasion of His power, presence, and purpose. As we've seen, awakening — revival — is where God does the unusual through unusual people at unusual times. A revived, Scripture-anchored Christianity is most certainly a surprise to those living in a run-of-the-mill, 98.6° F (as in a normal, average body temperature), cultural brand of religion.

> *"For I know that the Lord is great, and our Lord*
> *is above all gods. Whatever the Lord pleases He*
> *does, in heaven and in earth, in the seas and in*
> *all the deep places"* (Psalm135:5-7).

God does whatever, wherever, whenever, through whomever He pleases because — surprise — He is God! The sooner we get this, the better off we are.

# Chapter 7

# NO RISK, NO SURPRISE

From the very beginning, the young Hinkle family kept stepping out of the boat — directing Introduction Centers for girls coming off the street outside of New Orleans, in Mississippi and Phoenix, Arizona. These Introduction Centers with NLFG were the first phase of recovery in a program introducing the girls to Jesus and a new, Christ-centered life. Eventually we moved to Hollywood for a brief season, helping to relaunch the Holy Ghost Repair Service (now Oasis of Hollywood) reaching out to the broken and hurting on the streets of one of our nation's great mission fields.

While still living in California, I went to minister in the Dallas/

Ft. Worth area. While there, I visited some friends who worked for a large ministry that had a high-rise office building in Ft. Worth. Finding myself with some extra time, I went into the prayer room of the ministry and began to pray over the Dallas/Ft. Worth metroplex.

Upon returning home to Los Angeles, I began to feel impressed to move back to the Dallas area. I was resistant because of the love I had for the broken lives on the streets of Hollywood and how much Nancy and I enjoyed living in California. Yet, we yielded to the dealing of the Holy Spirit. The Hinkle family of four — Scott, Nancy and our children, Donovan and Stephanie — after only 15 months in California, began by faith to prepare for this monumental move, launching us deeper into the design God had for our lives.

When moving day came, we packed our belongings into a rented U-Haul truck. We had enough money and gas to go from the San Fernando Valley about 70 miles east to San Bernardino. This was a familiar situation for us — moving by faith across the country. While we were loading the truck, a man came and gave me $200. This was not enough to get to Texas but enough to get moving on the road. Off we went, heading to Texas. And once again, God provided miraculously along the way.

We knew it was time to launch a new evangelistic ministry —

Scott Hinkle Outreach Ministries. The word "outreach" was critical in defining our purpose and identity.

A house owned by a friend in the Dallas area had been made available for us at a monthly rental rate less than the cost for an apartment in Los Angeles. It was the first house we had ever lived in as a family, and we were overjoyed. With only one set of meetings scheduled, we launched out.

While driving the truck from California, the Lord spoke to me to take a team to Mardi Gras in New Orleans. The launching of this longtime outreach has made a dual impact. Hundreds of thousands of people who come to this city-wide celebration filled with drunkenness, perversion, and more, have heard the Gospel and many have come to Christ. In addition, God in His grace and power has taken what has been called a moral sewer and turned it into a training ground in evangelism for thousands of believers.

After arriving in Dallas, we did not have many open doors or invitations to hold revival meetings or speak in church services. I was feeling a bit depressed and was wondering what was happening. I felt called to preach the Gospel; yet, I was sitting at our dining room table staring at an empty calendar and the phone wasn't ringing. Clearly, I heard the Lord speak to my heart: *"They may not ask you to come — but I told you to GO!"*

Scott Hinkle Outreach Ministries was not forged in a denominational setting through church services or Christian youth camps but by going to the streets; leading outreaches to rock concerts; preaching in outdoor rallies on flatbed trucks; also at street meetings from Harlem to Hollywood Boulevard, at the Rose Bowl and Cotton Bowl parades; Florida's spring break; a citywide, multi-faceted outreach to Atlanta during the Democratic National Convention. There were numerous outreaches to urban, rural and suburban communities throughout America. Every imaginable setting where there were people to be reached was where we went.

Following an outreach to the Rose Parade in Pasadena, California, a handful of street ministers met at an outdoor taco stand to hear a bold, out-of-the-ordinary vision for a national conference to be held to train people to take Good News to the highways and byways of America and the world. It was something new, different, a bit crazy and yet desperately needed in the church world.

The plan was in place and the date was set for the very first National Street Ministries Conference. Much to the surprise of these street preachers and others, nearly 900 people from all types of ministries came to Dallas, Texas. David Wilkerson spoke for the final evening of our first conference. For twenty-three years, the National Street Ministries Conference (later known as A Passion for Souls), by God's grace, helped launch a fresh wave of frontline evangelism across America and in different parts of the world.

While many enter into ministry after being brought up in a Christian environment and following the typical church culture pattern, by His immeasurable love, grace and power, God continually raises up men and women from unreached and broken backgrounds, transforming them into vessels fit for the Master's use. This might even describe your path.

God takes shattered lives, puts them back together according to His purpose and plan and then entrusts them to use the same mending material, the gospel, in bringing His life to others.

> *"But God has chosen the foolish things of the world to confound the wise; and God has chosen the weak things of the world to confound the things which are mighty"* (1 Corinthians 1:27).

Paul, in talking about his own life, takes this point even further.

> *"And I thank Christ Jesus our Lord who has enabled me, because He counted me faithful, putting me into the ministry, although I was formerly a blasphemer, persecutor, and an*

55

*insolent man; but I obtained mercy because I did it ignorantly in unbelief. And the grace of our Lord was exceedingly abundant, with faith and love which are in Christ Jesus"* (1 Timothy 1:12-14).

# Section Three

# Chapter 8

# "A NEW THING"

I think everyone I know loves "new." A favorite verse for many of us, especially when a new year comes around is:

> "Do not [earnestly] remember the former things; neither consider the things of old. Behold, I am doing a new thing! Now it springs forth; do you not perceive it and know it and will you not give heed to it? I will even make a way in the wilderness and rivers in the desert" (Isaiah 43:18-19, AMPC).

God is most certainly into "new." He gives us a new day every morning; we become "new creations" (see 2 Corinthians 5:17); there will be new heavens and a new earth (see Isaiah 65:17); and we will even get a new name (see Revelation 2:17). That new name will be a great blessing for some of us who might be unhappy with the name we bear.

As excited as I get about new things — new year, new adventures, new home, new clothes, new sneakers or jeans, new cars (we like new so much we can even buy a used car and put a new car fragrance in it) — that is not what really captures my attention from Isaiah's words.

What stands out to me is the question: *"Do you not perceive it and know it and give heed to it?"*

## GETTING IT!

During a conversation with her husband, a wife, speaking from a womanly perspective, will look at him entrenched in male perspective and say, "You just don't get it, do you?" I really do want to get it, especially when it comes to my life with Jesus, don't you? I want to get hold of how God works in my life so He can do new things in me and even through me.

When God begins to do something new in my life, my initial response at times is that I am ready to launch into it immediately.

You make a few plans, outline a strategy, and jump out going for it. Right?

Then I discover there is one part of my being that is a bit slow to catch on — my thinking processes — my mind. When the Bible asks, "Do you not perceive it?" it cuts quite deep. In other words, God is asking, "Can you wrap your mind around the new thing I desire to do in and through you?"

The great part of the adventure of a life with Christ is really learning "how to get it." How to wrap our minds around and fully grasp everything new God desires to do and, moreover, get a bit more insight into how God is working in our life.

It can happen. God does not over promise and under deliver. The Word of God can renew your mind. It helps you and me get a grasp on God's workings and dealings a bit better.

> *"Be transformed by the renewing of your mind, that you may prove what is that good and acceptable and perfect will of God"* (Romans 12:2).

How good is that? God provides us the possibility of having our thought processes cleansed and made new!

This absolutely helps us to pursue, discover and fulfill God's will for our life, as well as become a bit more prepared for His surprises. Whether we came from what is called an unchurched background or were raised under a church pew, a "renewed mind" is essential to true fulfillment. A constant diet of God's Word in a daily devotional time, as well as in-depth study, can help cleanse and make your thinking new and in line with God. Paul speaks of this mind renewal process as a type of cleansing when he writes of being cleansed with the washing of water by the Word.

*"That He may sanctify and cleanse her with the washing of the water by the word"* (Ephesians 5:26).

I first experienced this water of the Word cleansing of my mind and thoughts early on in my newfound relationship with Jesus.

When I was a drug addict, I would view regular household items such as clock radios with an eye toward their value if I traded them for drugs on the streets. Immediately after coming to faith in Christ, I began to read the Bible. I found a version that was easy to read and understandable to me and the Holy Spirit began to work. I let it soak in and launch a massive cleanup job on some of my thoughts. The first time I walked into someone's home and saw a clock radio, I noticed the time and heard the music playing (incidentally, I didn't like the type of music I heard coming from it). I started to praise God because I realized He had begun to "renew my mind."

If you want this to take place, begin to regularly read God's Word. The best translation of the Bible is the one you can read, understand, and hear God speak through. It makes no difference whether it's the original Greek, Hebrew, Aramaic or a paraphrased version. A part of the Holy Spirit's job description is to teach us and lead us into truth.

> *"However, when He, the Spirit of truth, has come,*
> *He will guide you into all truth"* (John 16:13).

**Renewal through God's Word is an easy process — read it daily, believe it, apply it.**

# Chapter 9

# WHAT IS NORMAL?

It seems like everybody has something to say on this topic. From newscasters, to scientists and religious prognosticators, to celebrities to politicians — you name it. There are so many different answers that change from day to day, telling us what normal was, is now, and possibly will be in the future.

The dictionary says normal is *"the usual, average or typical state, degree, form"* (Free Dictionary). Besides the wide range of voices mentioned above, as well as the dictionary, when it comes to you and me, what is normal?

I am a Christ follower. My decision to follow Jesus was a personal one, made in a parking lot years ago. In my youth, my "normal, usual state of life" was scheming, stealing and being a heroin addict. But Jesus set me free from that and gave me a *new normal*!

With that decision, my frame of reference became one that was established from eternity past. If you and I share that same decision in following Christ, then we should probably share this same frame of reference — the Bible.

> *"The just shall live by faith"* (Habakkuk 2:4;
> Hebrews 10:38; Romans 1:17; Galatians 3:11).

Something written in the Scriptures not just once but four times tells us it is really important. It is such a radical truth that when preached by Martin Luther, it helped fuel the Reformation. God is underscoring a central, foundational truth, laying groundwork for all believers for what might be called "normal." Here it is: any normal — new or old — is dictated by what you *choose* to believe in your mind, heart and spirit!

I'm grateful to Matthew Barnett for sowing this thought into my thinking. Proverbs helps us as well:
> *"For as he thinks in his heart, so is he"* (Proverbs 23:7).

Consider the life of Abraham. He had a sure word and promise from God to *"become the father of many nations"* (Genesis 17:5). He was a hundred years old and his wife was ninety — and still no children. The Bible tells us,

> *"Against all hope, Abraham in hope believed and*
> *so became the father of many nations"* (Romans
> 4:18, NIV).

Joshua and Caleb saw the exact same things in the promised land that all the other spies saw. The ten spies gave a report discouraging God's children from taking possession of the land of Canaan that God said would be theirs. Caleb and Joshua saw the good, although they were not in denial about the giants and great challenges, either. Clearly, they used a different filter to process the situation, causing them to declare,

> *"Let us go up at once and take possession, for*
> *we are well able to overcome"* (Numbers13:30).

Who or what dictates what is normal to us as Christians? Is it the world, other people, sentiment, surroundings, circumstances or God and His Word?

You see, what we *choose* to believe determines new, old, or just plain regular normal in our lives. Abraham, Joshua and Caleb made the choice to put their trust in God and believe His word of promise, which determined what a normal course of action would be for them. The writer of Hebrews tells us,

*"So do not throw away this confident trust in the Lord. Remember the great reward it brings you!"* (Hebrews 10:35, NLT).

I cannot recall a time when our framework of reference — the belief system of our heart, mind, and spirit — needed to be more deeply and fully anchored in God's Word. Period!

*Let's make the commitment to allow the Word of God to dictate what is "normal." Let it begin this very moment and carry on into all of our tomorrows.*

# Chapter 10

# MY LIFE

*"It's my life*
*It's now or never*
*I ain't gonna live forever*
*I just wanna live while I'm alive*
*It's my life"*
> (*It's My Life,* lyrics by Jon Bon Jovi)

The words of this popular song ring ever so true, don't they? "I just wanna live while I'm alive." Life is what we are talking about. A fulfilled life, in fact.

The apostle Paul made a statement using the very same two words: "my life."

*"But my life is worth nothing to me unless I use it for finishing the work assigned me by the Lord Jesus — the work of telling others the Good News about the wonderful grace of God"* (Acts 20:24, NLT).

Paul's words, as is often the case, are pretty heavy. To say "my life is worth nothing to me" might appear to undercut the whole thrust of modern western culture. It does not. Much today is made of building and doing life; creating worth and value; living life. Life most certainly is a gift from God. It is to be developed, enjoyed, shared; it is filled with surprises and so much more, including fulfillment.

There can be no doubt whatsoever that any life — every life, our life, my life and your life — has immeasurable value. It's worth a great deal!

*Why?*

Simple.

Jesus Christ, God's only begotten Son, willingly gave up His own life (imagine the life Jesus must've had before coming to earth — no sin, sickness, pain, torment. *Wow!*) so that we could have real life *now* as well as throughout all eternity. It makes no sense, when you know the facts, to live life any other way but in and through Him. Wouldn't you agree?

According to God, every person ever born on this planet has worth and value exceeding any conceivable dollar amount. Regardless of parentage, ethnicity, heritage, bank account or community status, people have great value. In spite of our lives being reduced to passwords and PIN numbers, each and every person has an immeasurable worth.

Why? you might ask. That's easy. Each human being was fashioned and formed — created — in the image of God. Get this:

> *"Then God said, 'Let Us make man in Our image,*
> *according to Our likeness'"* (Genesis 1:26).

Being made in the image of God would bring limitless value to a life, wouldn't it? We often marvel and even display a bit of pride over how our children look and act like us. I believe God as our Father is pleased that His creation was made originally in His image. Yet, so many times I have encountered precious people who thought much less of themselves than God does. Through various circumstances and sometimes sin, they have lost any sense of dignity or self-worth. That is such a tragedy.

Once, while we were part of an inner-city outreach in a poverty-stricken community, a woman approached me and asked this question: "Is it all right if I come to this church?" For some reason, she thought I was the pastor. I could not believe my ears! I quickly began to ask myself, "What would cause her to be bold enough to ask such a thing?" I started to wonder, "Is she ashamed of her life for some reason?"

Maybe I was talking to a modern-day woman at the well, similar to the one Jesus spoke with (see John 4:7-26). I did not know why she asked this, but my answer to her was simple, compassionate, and direct: "We would love for you to come to this church." (By the time I answered, the pastor had come up beside me and echoed all that I said.) The very next day this lady and her two children came to church and she wept as the Holy Spirit powerfully touched her life.

Rest assured that your life is of infinite value to God. Never let anyone or anything tell you any different.

# Chapter 11

# THREE LIFE-DEFINING WORDS TO HELP YOU WALK THROUGH GOD'S SURPRISES

At a particularly crucial time in our life and ministry, I was preparing to preach a message to the church my wife Nancy and I had started and were pastoring in New Jersey. In the course of praying, studying and preparing, I realized there are three words that help us walk through God's surprises, define our walk with Jesus Christ, and even help us to connect with how God works in our lives. I believe they can be applied to you and your own life and help prepare you for the unexpected times you will most certainly encounter.

## PURPOSE

We have heard this first word very often these days but because we have heard it repeatedly does not diminish its value or indicate its loss of meaning to us.

It is the word *purpose*. Check out the definition of this often-used word: *"The reason for which something exists or is done, made, used"* (Dictionary.com).

When it comes to purpose in our lives, the bottom line is *we must know it!* This is God's stated desire for us.

> *"May He grant you according to your heart's desire, and fulfill all your purpose"* (Psalm 20:4).

The psalmist used the words "fulfill all your purpose." When God says all, He means *all!* Not 50 percent, 75 percent, or even 98 percent — but *all* 100 percent!

Have you ever wondered why you exist? I know I have. As a kid standing in our neighbor's driveway one night, looking up at all the stars and being a bit overwhelmed at the evening sky's expanse, I had some "God thoughts" even though, as a Jewish boy, I had no real interest in God or religion. My young mind was invaded by the overwhelming thoughts of "why" and "what."

The apostle Paul addresses the "why we exist" matter in the New Testament book of Romans:

> *"God knew what He was doing from the very beginning. He decided from the outset to shape the lives of those who love Him along the same lines as the life of His Son. The Son stands first in the line of humanity He restored. We see the original and intended shape of our lives there in Him"* (Romans 8:29-30, The Message).

Paul adds to this in his letter to the Colossians:

> *"We look at this Son and see the God who cannot be seen. We look at this Son and see God's original purpose in everything created"* (Colossians 1:15, The Message).

Our purpose in life can only truly be found in and through Jesus Christ. After all, the Bible tells us,

> *"He who has the Son has life; he who does not have the Son of God does not have life"* (1 John 5:12).

There are good reasons to get a grasp on life's purpose. Too many good people wander through life never fully connecting with God's intended design. They are missing some of the great surprises that are part and parcel of our lives in Christ. As

Christians, our primary purpose on this planet is to honor and glorify God, first and foremost. After all, He made us and gave us life, right?

Second, becoming like Jesus is certainly a purpose. In so many ways His life served as a pattern and example. Wouldn't you want to reflect Him to the world you live in?

Third, believe it or not, we are intended to do the things He did.

> *"Most assuredly, I say to you, he who believes in Me, the works that I do he will do also; and greater works than these he will do, because I go to My Father"* (John 14:12).

Having an understanding of your Bible-based purpose brings depth and meaning to your life, gets you started in the morning, and helps bring life into keener focus.

God spoke these words through Moses to Pharaoh:
> *"But indeed for this purpose I have raised you up, that I may show My power in you, and that My name may be declared in all the earth"* (Exodus 9:16).

If God had a purpose in raising up Pharaoh, how much greater purpose does He have for those who are His children.

Then there is Saul of Tarsus, who persecuted Christians. After he had that supernatural encounter with Jesus, knocking him off his horse to the ground, Jesus says to him,

> *"But rise and stand on your feet; for I have appeared to you for this purpose, to make you a minister and a witness both of the things which you have seen and of the things which I will yet reveal to you"* (Acts 26:16).

One more example. We read Daniel was a man of purpose:

> *"But Daniel purposed in his heart that he would not defile himself with the portion of the king's delicacies"* (Daniel 1:8).

Daniel illustrates how knowing your purpose will help you make the right choices and decisions to the point of avoiding what is detrimental to your well-being. Men and women of purpose are positioned for God's work and are prepared to experience His surprises in life.

If, per chance, you are reading this and you have never entered into a personal, living relationship with Jesus Christ, I urge you to do so — even now. Your life will change. It's not that difficult. This is not being said to get you to become religious or to simply acknowledge some philosophy or creed or become a member of an organization. This is an invitation for you to enter a life that God intended from eternity past for you to have now.

God's Word gives simple and clear instructions:

> *"If you confess with your mouth the Lord Jesus and believe in your heart that God has raised Him from the dead, you will be saved"* (Romans 10:9).

May I ask you this? Do you believe that when Jesus Christ died on the cross, He paid the penalty required by Law for the sins of every person of all times, including you and me? And when God raised Jesus from the dead, He proved that He could forgive our sins and give us a new life?

In addition, would you confess to God that you are a sinner and need His forgiveness, and exchange the life you have been living for the life He died to give you? This simple act will make you a child of God.

God does not want anyone to live their life only to perish apart from Him.

> *"The Lord is not slack concerning His promise, as some count slackness, but is longsuffering*

*toward us, not willing that any should perish but*
*that all should come to repentance"* (2 Peter 3:9).

Each God surprise has a purpose, and you and I should also. Knowing and understanding it is part of living in God's intended fullness.

## MISSION

The second word helping us to walk out God's surprises into a fuller dimension of His purpose is a word not uncommon to Christ followers. It is the word "mission." Merriam Webster's Collegiate Dictionary gives us a definition of this word: *"a ministry commissioned by a religious organization to propagate its faith or carry on humanitarian work."*

Let us look even further to how Jesus and the New Testament begin this concept of mission as it pertains to you and me.

In His conversation with the Father, Jesus says,
> *"As You sent Me into the world, I also have sent them into the world"* (John 17:18)

As Jesus stands before Pilate, He gives this response to the question, *"Are You a king then?"*

Jesus answered him,

> *"You say rightly that I am a king. For this cause*
> *I was born, and for this cause I have come into*
> *the world, that I should bear witness to the truth"*
> (John 18:37).

If you and I claim to be followers of Jesus, then He is referring to us as them! We are absolutely included here ... period. We, like Jesus, are to "bear witness to the truth."

Looking at some of the reasons Jesus came might help us uncover some purposes and missions God has for us.

> *"How God anointed Jesus of Nazareth with the*
> *Holy Spirit and with power, who went about doing*
> *good and healing all who were oppressed by the*
> *devil, for God was with Him"* (Acts 10:38).

This clearly lays it out. The mission of Jesus was about *"doing good"* and *"healing all who were oppressed of the devil."*

Doing good. If anyone calls you or your church a bunch of "do-gooders" tell them *thank you*! As a matter of fact, if you claim to be a Christian but are not doing any good for anyone else, what you possess may not be God-type, Bible-based faith. It may be some sort of religious froth but not Bible-based, proactive, people-helping, serving, reaching faith.

James 2:14-20:

> *"What does it profit, my brethren, if someone says he has faith but does not have works? Can faith save him? If a brother or sister is naked and destitute of daily food, and one of you says to them, 'Depart in peace, be warmed and be filled,' but you do not give them the things which are needed for the body, what does it profit? Thus also faith by itself, if it does not have works, is dead. But someone will say, 'You have faith, and I have works.' Show me your faith without your works, and I will show you my faith by my works ... But do you want to know, O foolish man, that faith without works is dead?"*

Picking up on Acts 10:38 again,

> *"Healing all who were oppressed of the devil."*

The modern-day application of this removes the potentially heavy religious interpretation. You may look at this as including alcoholics, drug addicts; the homeless, abused, neglected, abandoned; those having tormenting thoughts and self-destructive behavior; the feeling that you have been thrown under the bus of life every day. These would certainly qualify as being "oppressed," and moreover, would be the focus of the life-transforming power of Christ.

Jesus went around doing good and helping folks of all kinds who were all messed up. I would've been at the head of this line needing His help — how about you? We can follow His example.

Another integral part of "the mission" is wrapped up in John 10:10:

> *"The thief does not come except to steal, and to kill, and to destroy. I have come that they may have life, and that they may have it more abundantly."*

Part of the mission is "bringing life." I love the phrase being used to describe many churches today: "a life-giving church." There are one too many churches where there is not much life. People are unfriendly, you couldn't find a smile if you tried. Folks look like they've been baptized in lemon juice or are just plain mad at everything or everybody or both.

If you want to be a living testimony and reflect His life — smile! Maybe once a day for starters. The Bible gives us solid, spiritually legal and documentable reasons to have joy and smile. In fact, you cannot have joy and never smile.

Here are two of many of those reasons:

> *"Rejoice in the Lord always. Again I will say, rejoice!"* (Philippians 4:4).

> *"Rejoice because your names are written in heaven"* (Luke 10:20).

When you speak about Jesus forgiving your sins, don't talk in a mealy-mouth mumble; say it like you are grateful and mean it. Reflect a life that is filled with Christ's presence and not an empty-hearted, shallow religious imitation.

The Bible teaches:

> *"The joy of the Lord is your strength"* (Nehemiah 8:10).

I can never imagine Lazarus being raised from the dead and then walking out of the tomb griping and complaining about being raised up. He must have had a smile on his face.

Reflect the life of Christ to others. This most certainly is part of the mission we have. Believe it or not, our face can testify of God's love, grace, and power! We cannot give anyone life; only Jesus can but we can point people to His life, and in effect, plug people into Him.

Life on planet Earth is life in a constant spiritual war zone. We read,

> *"For this purpose the Son of God was manifested, that He might destroy the works of the devil"* (1 John 3:8).

Dealing with the devil is a definite part of the mission. Too many times when spiritual warfare is spoken of, people begin to get weird and spooky.

Primarily, there are three ways to engage in effective spiritual warfare:

1) Clean up your heart and life before God.

   *"If I regard iniquity in my heart, the Lord will not hear"* (Psalm 66:18).

   Having a heart and life that is clean before God gives solid ground on which to stand against the enemy. The legitimate cause for Satan to accuse you is then removed.

2) Engage the enemy through prayer and intercession. Holy Spirit-empowered worship would be included. There is a difference between empowered worship and just good music with religious lyrics.

3) Luke 19:10 tells us:

*"For the Son of Man has come to seek and to save that which was lost."*

One of the most fundamental ways to defeat Satan and his works in lives, families, communities and beyond is to lead people to Jesus Christ.

When a thief comes to Christ, there is less theft.

When a drug dealer gets saved, there are less drugs ruining people's lives.

When a crooked politician is genuinely converted, there is more righteous government activity.

When an abusive husband or wife gets saved, families are healed.

The principle carries forward.

Jesus went out of His way in leaving heaven and coming to earth to search after something God counts as His utmost work (and which had been lost to sin and destruction): mankind — men, women, teens and children all made in His image.

While discovering the purpose and mission for your life, it is best to follow in the footsteps of Jesus. Let me put it this way. Younger brothers or sisters often look up to their older siblings. They want to be like them, hang out with them, be with their friends and play with them. I'm the oldest of three boys and had this experience in childhood. My younger brother, Gary, wanted to be with me and play ball with the older guys. We sometimes let him play.

You can often nickname the younger brother or sister "Me Too" because they want to be with and follow in the footsteps of the older one. Jesus is our "elder brother." If you are endeavoring to lock into your purpose and mission, why not follow the example of your "elder brother" according to the Bible. Do the things that He did — become "me too" to Jesus.

Apply His purpose and mission to your life, draw from it, and allow it to become your purpose and mission. Remember His words to the Father in John 17:18:

> *"As you sent Me into the world, I also have sent them into the world."*

## ASSIGNMENTS

The third word that has helped to define my walk with Christ, seeing how He works in and through my life, is the word "assignments." This word helps unlock a whole new dimension of life and leads further to God's surprises. It's not really a Bible word that can be found in a concordance but there is a deeply rooted scriptural principle to be grasped.

> *"As they ministered to the Lord and fasted, the Holy Spirit said, 'Now separate to Me Barnabas and Saul for the work to which I have called them'"* (Acts 13:2).

God had specific assignments or work for Barnabas and Saul (Paul). This is seen clearly throughout the New Testament.

We read of David:

> *"After he had served his own generation by the will of God"* (Acts 13:36).

I believe this is saying David had fulfilled all his assignments. In a broad, sweeping sense, assignments are God's calls to us. But I want to get much more personal on this.

The definition of this word is *"a position, post, or office to which one is assigned: a specified task or amount of work assigned or undertaken as if assigned by authority"* (Merriam Webster's Collegiate Dictionary).

You and I have assignments to fulfill, so let's look at this some more.

*"The steps of a good man are ordered by the Lord, and He delights in his way"* (Psalm 37:23).

You see, God leads His people by steps, not major events or "big stuff." More on this point a bit later.

Throughout the course of my life, I have had many, many assignments. Whether you realize it or not, you have as well. Assignments come in many ways. For our thinking they can be broken down into three types: people, places and situations.

1) PEOPLE — My wife, Nancy, and our children are assigned to me. Some people are assigned to help you grow. Then there are those you are assigned to that they may be helped, encouraged, grow, advance. Friends are an assignment. God assigns people to your life for various purposes and reasons.

2) PLACES — If God directs your steps, He will lead you to places. Where you live, work, go to school, go on vacation and more. God can lead you into places for His purpose and to accomplish a part of His mission. As a travelling evangelist, I believe everywhere I minister, each church I speak in, is an assignment from God. There are certain towns, cities, regions or nations that are assignments to our life and ministry. We will partner with churches and ministries in different places

by assignment.

3) SITUATIONS — This may often be connected to being
   assigned to places. Reaching gang members through a
   special outreach in Phoenix was a short-term, event-
   based assignment. The Mardi Gras New Orleans
   Outreach is an assignment we've continued for years.

Jesus was a carpenter, and He custom builds assignments for
each of us. Our own personal assignments include equipping
more "Gospel spreaders" to reach their own world, as well as
our own mission to bring Good News to the inner cities.

I personally love standing in the midst of hurting, broken and
devastated humanity, calling them to Christ because He loves
them and will meet them wherever they are in life.

God has people, places and situations waiting just for you. Will
you grasp this in your heart and mind?

Some assignments are short-term. It may be the seat assignment
you are given on an airline that places you next to someone you
are destined to share Christ with. It may be something more
long-term, but nevertheless, both are divine assignments that
may also put you in the realm of divine surprises if you follow
through.

Let me be very plain. When your life has been bought with a price, it is no longer your own.

*"For you were bought at a price; therefore glorify God in your body and in your spirit, which are God's"* (1 Corinthians 6:20).

*"Therefore take heed to yourselves and to all the flock, among which the Holy Spirit has made you overseers, to shepherd the church of God which He purchased with His own blood"* (Acts 20:28).

When you choose to follow Christ, no longer can you sing the song "It's My Life," because it is not. Your life has been purchased — bought and paid for — through the death and blood of Jesus Christ.

It may come as a shock, but really, we fully belong to Him. Therefore, we should be available for His assignments. I repeat: He bought and paid for our lives, which gives Him the right to call the shots and give directions.

As we align ourselves with His clearly defined, scriptural purpose and mission, we are in position to receive His personalized, made-just-for-us assignments. Often divine assignments begin as seeds sown into our heart by the Holy Spirit.

Assignments or God-birthed visions are progressive; as they begin to unfold and grow, they will progress, taking on greater shape and fulfilling a longer-range purpose. They might come as simple ideas or thoughts or even through a Scripture. As small and insignificant as they might seem, they may unfold into an action or assignment.

> *"It is like a mustard seed, which is the smallest of all seeds on earth. Yet when planted, it grows and becomes the largest of all garden plants, with such big branches that the birds can perch in its shade"* (Mark 4:31-32, NIV).

God-birthed assignments may often be birthed like this. Understand, some assignments in life are primarily for your benefit, designed for you to be a vessel of help and blessing to others. Yet so many assignments are mutually beneficial for others and you!

Are there causes, calls or assignments in your own life that have been sidestepped, neglected or lie dormant? Now is the time for pursuit.

Our pursuit must be intentional!

Surprises frequently happen to those who are set up for them.

*"Ask, and it will be given to you; seek, and you will find; knock, and it will be opened to you"* (Matthew 7:7).

God responds to those who intentionally go after Him and His direction for their lives. He is lovingly waiting to set you up for surprises through the purposes, mission, and assignments He has for you. Understand, your assignments are not based upon your current life status, situation, talents or lack of them, but on the potential you have in and through Christ alone.

*"I can do all things through Christ who strengthens me"* (Philippians 4:13).

The obvious emphasis is *"through Christ."*

Once again, our purpose and mission are clearly established, and might I add, are nonnegotiable. Are you desiring and ready for God's assignments? Some assignments in life are renewed year after year. This may be hard, but some will run their course and need to phase out or simply end. You cannot move on to a new assignment if you are locked into one whose time has passed.

Of course, as long as we are on this planet, there will be new assignments.

Are you ready?

# Chapter 12

# BECOMING AN AGENT OF CHANGE

*"Jesus knew that his mission was now finished, and to fulfill Scripture he said, 'I am thirsty.' A jar of sour wine was sitting there, so they soaked a sponge in it, put it on a hyssop branch, and held it up to his lips. When Jesus had tasted it, he said, 'It is finished!' Then he bowed his head and gave up his spirit"* (John 19:28-30, NLT).

When Billy Graham passed away at the age of ninety-nine, he could have spoken the words of Jesus, "It is finished."

Although his ministry continues beyond the span of his life, his personal assignments had been completed. He had run his race, he had completed his own mission.

When Reinhard Bonnke passed away at seventy-nine, he too could have said, "It is finished," regarding the assignments heaven personally entrusted him with. He had completed his mission as well.

Please understand, if I were sitting across from you right now, looking into your eyes, I would have to tell you from the depths of my heart, *"It is not finished!"*

There is much to be done, and the need for those who will be about the Father's business in our broken world is greater than ever. That is part of the reason for this book.

A word is at the heart of what must take place — a word that excites some people, moving them ahead in life or strikes fear in others, terrifying and paralyzing them. It produces action or resistance.

This word is *change*. Without a doubt, change is part of what life is all about on planet Earth.

During election time, many candidates run on the platform of change. We may cast a vote hoping for change. We move to a different location, get a new job or even go to a different church looking for change.

From the moment we are conceived and throughout our earthly life, change occurs in our body and overall being.

I've discovered that Christ followers are intended to be "agents of change." Actually, the people of God are intended to be the greatest agents of change on the Earth today. Let's take a look at some background on this.

Change is an integral part of real Christianity. When Jesus came on the scene, religion, as it was known then, was changed forever! When Jesus Christ makes his home in your heart, there is change:

> *"Then Christ will make his home in your heart as*
> *you trust in him"* (Ephesians 3:17, NLT).

When you move into a new house, condo or apartment, you bring in your furniture, pictures, decorative pieces, household items, and you arrange them to suit yourself. You may even make some improvements or install new carpet and paint. It's the same when Christ comes in. As a matter of fact, if there has been no change since a person has claimed to "accept Christ," then it is highly possible that they have had some kind of religious encounter or emotional experience but Christ did not make entry into their life.

A personal encounter with the Jesus of the Bible lovingly yet firmly demands change. You cannot encounter the Savior without change occurring. After all, forgiveness, cleansing, healing and deliverance are all connected to God-type change! Taking a mere human from darkness to light; death to life; old life to new life can be called nothing but CHANGE!

Christianity, the gospel, and the church are to be "transformative" in nature, practice, fruit and evidence. The word transformative means *"causing a marked change in something or someone"* (Oxford Dictionary).

The Bible speaks clearly about change:
> *"But the path of the righteous is like the light of dawn that shines brighter and brighter until the full day"* (Proverbs 4:18, NASB).

This sounds very much like change.

> *"We shall not all sleep, but we shall all be changed"* (1 Corinthians 15:51).

This tells us that in the final time, at the end of life, we shall be changed.

> *"Do not remember the former things, nor consider*

*the things of old. Behold, I will do a new thing,*
*now it shall spring forth; shall you not know it?*
*I will even make a road in the wilderness and*
*rivers in the desert"* (Isaiah 43:18-19).

Scripture tells us to recognize and embrace change. It's desperately needed.

Did you experience a change when Christ came into your life? I sure did and still am.

I would venture a guess that you would agree with me that our world, nation, community, and people we know all need change. Right?

Here is a big surprise. The greatest agents of change in our nation are not the President of the United States, a governor, mayor, or city councilman but the people of God — that's you and me!

It is quite interesting that with the knowledge of all the earthly elements, the Co-Creator of the Universe, Jesus, chose two common elements to describe the lives of His followers: salt and light. These two elements effect change with whatever they come in contact with and because He calls us salt and light, we should have this effect, as well.

# Chapter 13

# AN OPEN LETTER TO CONTEMPORARY AMERICAN EVANGELISTS (MYSELF INCLUDED)

The office of evangelist is an equally important part of the Ephesians 4:11 and 12 listing of the five-fold ministry gifts. Stirring up, edifying the Body, equipping for evangelism — these most certainly define the legitimate role of the evangelist to the church.

Without a doubt, every Christ follower should share their faith with others, regardless of other gifts or callings they possess. Yet it must be clearly understood, the great distinctive to the gift/office of evangelist is their calling to be the clear voice to the lost, declaring the gospel and calling them to Christ.

The other offices listed in Ephesians 4:11-12 are church oriented, being both inward and infrastructure focused. The evangelist should be focused upon the outside world at large where the unsaved and unchurched live.

If that be true, why then is there amongst some evangelists a seemingly inordinate amount of energy spent in complaining about a perceived lack of recognition by other church leaders? As if other church leaders determine the call of God.

Would the effort and energy be better invested prayerfully, and even creatively, looking for ways to invade the darkness outside the four walls of church buildings, instead of concentrating on, and at times whining about, what is perceived as a lack of acknowledgement from peers? Or does the contemporary version of the American evangelist seek validation by being invited to preach primarily in Christian gatherings, or put it another way, fish in bathtubs?

*The great evangelists of history — both old and new — risked venturing into deep waters, and at times unsafe stormy seas, to be fishers of men.*

Would not those be great models to follow after if our hearts truly were consumed with a passion to make Christ known to the least and fully lost men, women and children of our times? This necessitates leaving the safe harbor of "churchdom" and, to quote the great missionary evangelist T.L. Osborn, going *"out where the sinners are."*

This letter does not come from a critical spirit but from a soul crying out on behalf of a broken culture and dying world. The darkness of our era is desperate for the light of Christ. Now, more than ever, there must be another great awakening.

*This is a call to not only raise the bar higher for evangelists but to extend a challenge to drastically expand the horizons of our perspective, vision, and practice.*

I pray great grace to all sharing Good News.

# Chapter 14

# MORE, MORE, MORE

During the early days of this COVID-19 pandemic, restaurants here in Dallas were providing only drive-through, take-out service. Nancy and I were hungry for some barbeque, so I went to pick up some for dinner. When I arrived at the restaurant, there was a long wait in the pick-up line. I must admit, seeing that line and knowing I'd have to wait wasn't very encouraging.

As I made slow progress and waited in the line, a simple question popped into my mind: *"What is our post-pandemic plan?"* Almost immediately a thought exploded in my spirit and it was this: To preach MORE GOSPEL to MORE PEOPLE in MORE PLACES!

*It was a simple answer to a simple question.* There is an overwhelming need for this in practically every level of life, and in society and humanity as a whole. Would you agree that the greatest human need shared by every human being ever born is to hear the gospel of Jesus Christ in order to be reconciled to our loving God?

This radical, life-transforming message must be presented in a direct and clear way under the anointing of the Holy Spirit. Only then can someone make the decision to surrender their life to the One Who gave His life, paying the required price for everything wrong — every sin — you and I have ever committed in action, words or thought.

Once a person is forgiven and freed from the bondage of sin, the issues of the heart — bitterness, anger, rejection, hatred and more — can be overcome. This potentially creates a pathway to address many of society's problems which all — believe it or not — have their root in the sin in a man or woman's heart.

This is what happened to me and I trust it has been your experience as well.

> *"For out of the heart proceed evil thoughts, murders, adulteries, fornications, thefts, false witness, blasphemies"* (Matthew 15:19).

While this might appear to be overly simple, it's true! What we see happening in our land and world is born out of the evil and sin in our heart.

Yet we are also told,
> *"If we confess our sins, he is faithful and just and will forgive us our sins and purify us from all unrighteousness"* (1 John 1:9, NIV).

There must be a move among us to spread MORE GOSPEL to MORE PEOPLE in MORE PLACES!

The gospel of Jesus Christ is God's laser-beamed weapon, focused on the bull's eye of our primary problem ... sin.

The apostle Paul's words strike at our heart:
> *"For I am not ashamed of the gospel of Christ, for it is the power of God to salvation for everyone who believes: for the Jew first and also for the Greek"* (Romans 1:16).

*There must be a move amongst us to spread* MORE GOSPEL to MORE PEOPLE in MORE PLACES!

# Chapter 15

# THERE IS NO ONE ELSE

*"So I sought for a man among them who would
make a wall, and stand in the gap before Me on
behalf of the land, that I should not destroy it; but
I found no one"* (Ezekiel 22:30).

Isn't it difficult to comprehend that the God of all creation who
is omnipotent, omnipresent and omniscient could not find one
person for one task or assignment? Having served as a pastor,
I know what it's like to need one more greeter, or an additional
worker in the nursery. In leading numerous outreaches, you
may look for one more team member or van driver. The fact of
God not being able to find one person is hard to imagine — yet
it occurred.

God is looking for someone for a particular assignment. There is no one He would rather use than you. You are what He's looking for — surprise!

We read:

> *"For many are called, but few are chosen"* (Matthew 22:14).

The "choosing" may often depend upon your response to the call. If you refuse, He may look for someone else. How will you respond to His calling?

The call may be to go across the street — or around the world. It may be to speak to a grocery store cashier you see often or to a great crowd of thousands.

There is no one else who prays like you pray.

There is no one else who worships like you worship.

There is no one else who cares about others as you care about others.

There is no one else who serves as you serve. Surprise!

There is no one else who can respond to God's call and

assignments as you do.

Let God make you His surprise to your family, your community, and the world!

# ABOUT THE AUTHOR

Scott Hinkle, an evangelist now headquartered in Dallas, Texas, lived a life that pointed in only one direction — prison and ultimately an early grave. In an outdoor parking lot, someone witnessed to Scott and his life was drastically rearranged as he experienced the life-transforming power of Jesus Christ.

Today, this one-time Jewish heroin addict, raised on the Jersey Shore, is leading a charge with a direct and radical message that is having a profound effect on the Kingdom of God across our nation. He is known for his practical, challenging, and sometimes humorous, Bible-based messages.

Scott, along with his wife Nancy, founded Scott Hinkle Outreach Ministries. A grassroots revolution began through their National Street Ministries Conferences (A Passion for Souls), which trained and ministered to thousands of evangelistic workers, leaders, and pastors.

An author of three books, Scott has also written a column for *Charisma* magazine. He has been a church planter, served as a senior pastor, an adjunct teacher of evangelism in three Bible colleges, and developed a groundbreaking Bible college training program for evangelism.

Beyond conducting rallies, outreaches, and conferences, Scott and Nancy lead an annual multifaceted evangelistic invasion of the Mardi Gras celebration in New Orleans. Their ministry continually stretches internationally across social, age and cultural lines.

Scott and Nancy are married with two children. They are both graduates of Christ For The Nations Institute and are ordained ministers.

Contact Scott at:

**Scott Hinkle Outreach Ministries**

P.O. Box 1093

Midlothian, Texas 76065


www.scotthinkle.org

Made in the USA
Middletown, DE
03 November 2020

23251722R00062